Word Wise

Vol. Two

Alison Brown

THE BANNER OF TRUTH TRUST

THE BANNER OF TRUTH TRUST
3 Murrayfield Road, Edinburgh EH12 6EL, UK
P.O. Box 621, Carlisle, PA 17013, USA

*

© Alison Brown 2012

*

ISBN: 978 1 84871 178 5

*

Typeset in Arial 16/19 & 18/21 at
The Banner of Truth Trust,
Edinburgh

Printed in the USA by
Versa Press Inc.
East Peoria, IL.

*

*Dedicated to my son Nathanael,
whose excitement in childhood at finding
science in the Bible made me long
to share it with other children.*

Famous People

Many people today think that because the Bible is a very old book it must be rather out of date. They imagine that it is simply a collection of stories which have nothing to teach us about the universe we live in!

But some of the most respected scientists in history thought differently. They were amazed at the perfection they found in nature. They were convinced that there had to be a designer behind all the perfectly working systems which combine to make our world. They believed the designer was God and that the Bible was his Word.

Galileo, (who invented the first telescope for looking at stars) wrote the following words... 'The book of nature is a book written by the hand of God in the language of mathematics.'*

Using an encyclopedia can you match these Bible-believing scientists to the discoveries or inventions they became famous for?

James Simpson	Penicillin
Louis Pasteur	Antiseptic
Lord Joseph Lister	The Telegraph
Michael Faraday	Vaccination
Samuel F.B. Morse	Law of Gravity
Isaac Newton	Chloroform
Alexander Fleming	Electric Generator

see page 32

God the Designer

Some of those early scientists also believed that they would get to know more about God if they looked very carefully at the things he had made.

As they studied the colours, structures and processes in nature they kept finding beautifully balanced patterns! They could see that the designer was a God who loved orderliness.

The word 'science' comes from a latin word 'scientia', which means 'knowledge'. The Bible states that, **'The fear of the Lord is the beginning of knowledge'. (Proverbs 1:7)** Knowledge begins when we recognize who God is!

Unscramble the words below to make true sentences.

Early to learn wanted more scientists God about

....

They made God things the wonderful had looked carefully at

....

They beautifully patterns kept balanced finding

....

The 'scientia' word 'knowledge' latin means

....

Knowledge we recognize is begins when God who

....

Earthly Things

The Bible is God's **message** to the world, which he wants **everyone** to read. It **teaches** us about God himself, and his Son, the Lord Jesus Christ. But it also has much to say about the **physical** world we live in. Biblical descriptions of **earthly** things, are still perfectly **accurate**. Bible statements about scientific issues have **never** been proved wrong, in spite of their **age**. Some scientists have made a new **discovery** and then found that it was **already** described in God's Word!

2 Peter 1:21 says ....

....

....

....

The words written in bold letters are hidden in the wordsearch. Can you find them?

Y	R	E	V	O	C	S	I	D	A
A	M	L	A	C	I	S	Y	H	P
K	E	G	L	E	L	M	O	R	E
O	S	V	R	T	E	L	N	I	R
E	S	N	E	A	R	T	H	L	Y
D	A	G	A	R	D	U	I	S	R
E	G	A	D	U	Y	B	A	T	E
F	E	R	Y	C	I	O	B	A	V
A	T	S	O	C	L	H	N	S	E
S	E	H	C	A	E	T	A	E	N

Earth's Foundations

The Bible has much to say about how God created the earth. Since God alone knew what earth's size, shape and purpose would be, he is the only one who would know how to make the foundations! Foundations keep a building in the right place . . . and Earth is still orbiting the sun!

When God was talking with a man called Job, what question did God ask him? (**Job 38:4-6**) ....

....

....

....

....

Match each scripture reference below to the truth it teaches.

God is everlasting. He has neither beginning nor end.

Isaiah 40:28

God understands everything. He is never tired or weary.

Psalm 90:2

God created the earth to be inhabited.

Isaiah 45:18

In **Isaiah 48:13** God says ....

....

....

....

Measurements

Colour the beginning and end of each sentence to match.

1. Hundreds of measurements had to be just right...

2. Earth's distance from the sun is just one...

3. If Earth was a little further from the sun...

4. If Earth was closer to the sun its...

5. The Bible teaches that it...

...surface would be scorched!

...example of its perfect design.

...was God alone who did all the measuring!

...to make Earth a place where life would be possible.

...it would be a frozen, barren wasteland!

Write the beautiful words of **Isaiah 40:12-13** here....................................

....

....

....

....

....

....

Hanging on Nothing

Job 26:7 says ....

....

....

Down through the centuries various ancient myths and legends have suggested that the earth was (elhd) .... up by a giant called Atlas, or supported by elephants, huge columns, or a turtle! But the writer of the (okbo) .... of Job stated that the earth hangs upon nothing.

Job is (eon) .... of the oldest books in the Bible, and was probably written around the (meit) .... of Abraham, which was about 2000 years (febore) .... Christ.

Yet the words used by the writer of Job describe what we now (wkno) .... to be true! Earth is not propped up by an object or an animal, but is held in its orbit around the (nus) .... by a powerful (fcoer) .... which we now call gravity.

To (ays) .... that the earth 'hangs upon nothing' is a wonderful way to describe a world which is simply suspended in (cpsae) .... Only God could be holding it there!

Around the World

During the 15th century many people believed that the **world** was **flat**. In fact they thought that if they sailed too near the **edge** they might fall off and be lost for ever!

In 1519 AD a Portuguese sailor named **Magellan** left **Spain**, to sail to the Spice Islands (in Indonesia). He believed that the earth was a **sphere** and that the journey would be shorter if his fleet sailed westward rather than eastward. It was a **long** and dangerous **voyage,** round the tip of South America, and most of the crew died. Magellan himself died too before one of his ships finally arrived safely back to Spain in 1522.

There were only 18 starving men left on board, but they had, in fact, sailed right around the world!

Did you know that God's Word was completed over a thousand years earlier ….but that it stated, long **before** Magellan, that the earth was **round**! (Isaiah 40:22)

Can you fit the words in bold letters into the grid?

Earth is a Sphere

Isaiah 40:22 (talking about God) says: ....
....
....
....

If (1,1) =A, (2,1) =B, (3,1) =C etc. can you fill in the missing words?

No matter where we go the changing horizon in front of us reminds us that (5,1)(1,1)(3,4)(5,4)(3,2) .... is a sphere. We know that we are travelling around on the surface of a (2,1)(1,1)(2,3)(2,3) .... If we look at other (1,4)(2,3)(1,1)(4,3)(5,1)(5,4)(4,4) .... through a powerful telescope we will find that they too have a similar rounded shape. English Bible translators used the word 'circle' because the Hebrew language had only (5,3)(4,3)(5,1) .... word for both 'circle' and 'sphere'. When we find scientific facts described in the Bible like this we are (3,4)(5,1)(3,3)(4,2)(4,3)(4,1)(5,1)(4,1) .... that the Bible was inspired by the (3,1)(3,4)(5,1)(1,1)(5,4)(5,3)(3,4) ....

5	U	V	W	X	Y
4	P	Q	R	S	T
3	K	L	M	N	O
2	F	G	H	I	J
1	A	B	C	D	E
	1	2	3	4	5

Day and Night

Because the earth is spherical (or ball-shaped) and is constantly rotating or spinning on its axis, only the .... which is facing the sun will have daylight. When the area you live in is on Earth's dark side, away from the ...., then you will probably be in your bed, and sound asleep!

In the New Testament Jesus spoke about the moment of his return. He explained that it would happen ...., and without any warning.

In **Luke 17:26-36** Jesus said that when he returns some people will be out working in the .... during the day, while others are sleeping in their ...., during the night.

This is because God's Word is speaking about a spherical world where both day and night are taking place at the .... time. The Bible is completely reliable. It doesn't have any ....

2 Timothy 3:16a says.........................

....

....

....

....

Glory in the Sky

Earth is only a very small part of a huge solar-system. Each of the **planets** is moving around the sun on a different **path** and at a different speed. There are also travelling **comets** and asteroids. Astronomers can map their courses and work out **exactly** where each one will be in a year's time! Only God could have arranged the balance and **timing** of such a huge **system** and only God can keep it all **working** perfectly!

When David was writing the Psalms about 3000 years ago, he may not have understood as much as we do about astronomy. But the **more** we learn about the planets and **stars** the more we understand how very **true** David's words were!

Can you fit the words in bold letters into the grid?

Psalm 19:1 says ....

....
....
....
....
....
....
....
....

The Moon

Nowadays we don't (14,15,20,9,3,5) .... moonlight nearly as much as people did years ago! We have electric lighting in our homes and (2,1,20,20,5,18,25) .... powered headlamps on our cars. We can travel long distances in the (4,1,18,11) ...., and never stop to question how bright the moon is!

Long ago people needed (13,15,15,14,12,9,7,8,20) .... when they went out at night. Country meetings were arranged to take place on the night of a 'full moon' so that everyone would be able to (20,18,1,22,5,12) .... safely.

The time taken for the moon to change shape, from a (20,8,9,14) .... crescent to a full circle, and back again, is called a lunar month. The word 'month' comes from an old English (23,15,18,4) .... meaning 'moon'.

By watching the lunar month farmers knew when to (19,15,23) ....their seed or gather their animals in. Their (3,1,12,5,14,4,1,18) .... was based on the changing shape of the moon. The Bible, in **Psalm 104:19**, describes this (5,24,1,3,20,12,25) ....

Psalm 104:19 says ....

....

13

How many Stars?

Johannes **Kepler** was a German **astronomer** who lived between 1571 and 1630 AD. Like many people before him Kepler was keen to discover just how many **stars** there were in the sky. After careful **counting** he listed a **total** of 1005. He also helped to develop more powerful **telescopes** to allow astronomers to see much further into space.....but the further they could see, the **more** stars they found! Today we know that there are over 100 **billion** stars in our own galaxy and at least 100 billion other galaxies!

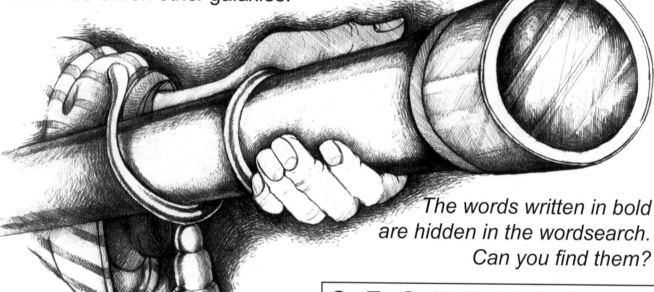

The words written in bold are hidden in the wordsearch. Can you find them?

It took astronomers hundreds of years to discover something about the stars that Bible writers already **knew**. Today astronomers **agree** that the stars cannot be counted.

Jeremiah 33:22a says..........

....
....
....
....

C	T	S	U	B	V	S	O	W	R
O	K	A	R	I	T	E	N	E	S
U	E	B	A	L	T	P	M	N	B
N	P	E	M	L	G	O	L	K	A
T	L	U	W	I	N	C	T	G	M
I	E	R	S	O	U	S	R	A	I
N	R	O	R	N	I	E	P	U	L
G	I	T	A	O	E	L	I	N	S
O	S	L	T	W	P	E	R	O	M
A	W	E	S	F	E	T	A	V	T

Star Variety

1 Corinthians 15:41 says

....
....
....
....
....
....
....
....
....

Long before the telescope was invented, the Bible also stated that stars were all different. Some stars appear yellow, like the sun. Some seem almost blue or red. There is great variety in their colour and brightness because they all have differing sizes and temperatures. Stars are shining continually, but we can only see them when the sky is dark!

Some questions to answer...

Which came first, the Bible or the telescope?
....

Using telescopes, what have we discovered about stars?
....

Why are stars different in brightness and colour?
....

Why do we only think about stars at night?
....

Why can we always trust Bible statements?
....

Guiding Lights

The Bible explains why God put the sun, moon and **stars** in the sky. As well as providing light they were to be like **signs,** which would help the wandering travellers on earth have some idea of their location.

Genesis 1:14 says ....

....

....

....

Years ago sailors had only the moon and stars to keep them from getting lost at **sea**. The North star serves as a **guide** to the direction north because it always appears to be directly above the North Pole.

Sailors also used the positions of very bright stars, like **Sirius**, **Canopus, Arcturus** or **Vega** and well known star groups such as **Orion**, and **Pleiades**,(mentioned in Job 9:9) to chart their course through unknown waters.

Can you fit the words in bold letters into the grid?

The Wind

Today we know that wind is caused by uneven heating of the atmosphere. The air above the hot parts of the earth, near the equator, expands and rises, and then cooler air flows in to replace the heated air. We also know that air circulates between the equator and the two poles, and that the wind follows certain known circuits. Centuries before the birth of Jesus, King Solomon wrote about the movement of the wind and his words still remain perfectly accurate.

New discoveries about our wonderful world always agree with what we find in the Bible.

Ecclesiastes 1:6 says ....
....
....
....
....

Can you rearrange these words to make true statements about the wind?

The of caused wind by uneven the atmosphere is heating
....

Air two and circulates the between equator the poles
....

We follows that certain wind know circuits the known
....

Solomon about in Ecclesiastes the book wrote wind of the
....

Refilling Rivers

Ancient people used to watch all the great rivers flowing from the land down into the sea and then wonder why the sea level didn't rise! Where did **all** that water **go**? Why didn't the sea get **deeper** and cover all the land? Where did all the **rain** come from in the first place? It wasn't until the 1500s that scientists began to understand just what was happening and the idea of a water cycle was accepted.

Can you fit the words in bold letters into the grid?

The reason why the oceans don't get much deeper is because the heat of the sun causes their waters to **evaporate**. Sea water is salty but the salt is left behind as the water rises up into the air in vapour. When the vapour cools, it condenses to form **clouds** of water droplets (just like when warm steam hits your cold bathroom mirror). Clouds later lead to rainfall, which eventually **fills** the rivers up again! That's why the earth never runs out of moisture. Water is simply used **over** and over again in a never-ending water cycle....just as we read in Ecclesiastes 1:7

The Water Cycle

Ecclesiastes 1:7 says ....
....
....
....

This verse is believed to have been written by wise King **Solomon**, about 2500 years before the idea of a water **cycle** was recognised! It clearly states that the **seas** don't fill up too deeply because the water **returns** back to where the **rivers** first **began**! God's Word is simply **describing** what happens when water evaporates, condenses to form **clouds** and then rains down again to **refill** the rivers. God designed it all in the first place!

```
L L I F E R C B J G
A U S N R U T E R N
C L O U D S O I E I
L O L E N S V R G B
S W O R D E I C A I
A E M H R B U Y E R
E U O S U E R C C C
S K N I O G U L A S
A D E T S A W E L E
D L R O W N O N P D
```

The words written in bold letters are hidden in the wordsearch. Can you find them?

Raindrops

Job 36:27-28 says ....
....
....
....

We have already noted that the book of (obJ) .... is one of the (dsloet) .... parts of the Bible. Yet it gives another very (elrca) .... description of the (ayw) ....water is drawn up as vapour which then condenses, or distills, to form clouds of (elttli) ....water droplets. When these fall back down on the earth we call it (anir) ....

Isn't it amazing how the writer of Job, inspired by God the Holy Spirit, gave details of this scientific (rhtut)................, even though he lived so very (ognl) .... ago?

You will find more words about the water cycle in **Amos 9:6b**. Write them here ....
....
....

Water to Drink

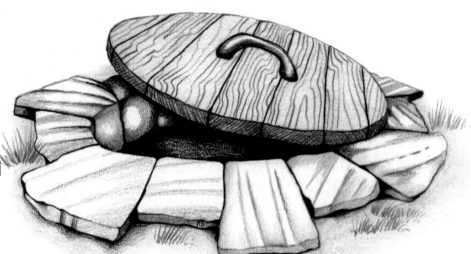

The book of Leviticus was written by Moses about 3500 years ago. It contains some laws given by God which would set his people apart from others. God wanted them to live holy and healthy lives.

In **Leviticus 11:29-36** we read that the Hebrews were instructed not to drink water which had been in contact with meat or dead animals. Certain kinds of bacteria found in dead and decaying bodies could cause very serious disease. Disease in the water would spread very quickly to all the people who were using it daily in their homes!

Down through history thousands of people have died due to diseases, which can be carried in water. More recently doctors have understood how this happens and just how vital clean drinking water is. But God's instruction on the matter was recorded in Scripture much, much earlier!

Some questions to answer...

Why did God want to give the Hebrews laws like this?
....

Why would it be wise to have a lid on a village well?
....

Why would an unclean water supply be very dangerous?
....

Why does God know so much about people and their health?
....

A Place to Live

Choose a word from the list to fill each blank space below.

Just consider how absolutely perfect planet Earth is for us to .... on. We have an atmosphere in which we can comfortably breathe. We have precisely the right amount of oxygen to keep ourselves and our .... healthy, but enough carbon dioxide to keep plants alive as well. Without plants we would ....! We have enough warmth and enough water for survival. We have seasons for growth and seasons for harvest. We have regular times of darkness in which to .... our bodies. If any .... of these things was to change, even a little, the result would be widespread illness or .... The Bible states that God ....

the earth for a special reason. That's why it's very .... from the other planets!

You'll find the reason in **Isaiah 45:18** ....
....
....
....
....
....
....
....
....
....
....

In the Right Order

Have you ever thought about (awht) .... is needed for plants to be able to grow strong and healthy? All plants (ened) .... air, sunlight and (tarew) ....

But these on their own are not enough. They also need minerals and nutrients which they usually get from the (iols) .... they are planted in.

Everyone (onksw) .... that if any of these are lacking the (tpaln) .... will soon begin to wither and die.

In **Genesis chapter 1** we read that first God created (gtilh) ...., then water, then soil, and *finally* plants. He didn't make any living things until he knew that they would be (leba) .... to survive on the earth. What we know to be (rteu) .... in the natural world is in agreement with the order of creation that we find in Scripture.

Check Genesis chapter 1 and decide which came first...

whales or water (.......................)   sunshine or people (..................)

monkeys or bananas (......................)   cows or grass (................)

people or vegetables (......................)   otters or fish (..................)

carrots or rabbits (.......................)   worms or soil (................)

oceans or dolphins (......................)   trees or birds (................)

Life in a Seed

Genesis 1:11 says ....

....

....

If (1,1) =A, (2,1) =B, (3,1) =C etc. can you fill in the missing words?

A seed is a wonderful thing. It (3,1)(5,3)(4,3)(5,4)(1,1)(4,2)(4,3)(4,4)
.... all the information needed to make a fully grown plant.
It determines the plant's size, leaf shape and (3,1)(5,3)(2,3)(5,3)(1,5)(3,4)
.... as well as the beautiful (4,1)(5,1)(4,4)(4,2)(2,2)(4,3)
.... and (1,4)(5,1)(3,4)(1,2)(1,5)(3,3)(5,1) .... of the flowers.

If seeds are pollinated and have a suitable place to (2,2)(3,4)(5,3)(3,5)
.... they will germinate to produce a (4,4)(3,2)(5,3)(5,3)(5,4) ....
and a (3,4)(5,3)(5,3)(5,4) .... before developing into a fully
formed plant. Scientists have tried to change seeds but they have *never*
managed to make a seed all by themselves. The amazing seed is still
as it was (1,4)(5,1)(3,4)(1,2)(5,1)(3,1)(5,4)(2,3)(5,5) ....
described in the Bible. **Genesis 1:11** states that every plant will produce
seed within itself, after its own
(1,3)(4,2)(4,3)(4,1) ....
Acorns, today, *still* grow into
(5,3)(1,1)(1,3) .... trees!

5	U	V	W	X	Y
4	P	Q	R	S	T
3	K	L	M	N	O
2	F	G	H	I	J
1	A	B	C	D	E
	1	2	3	4	5

Seeds must Die

Colour the beginning and end of each sentence to match...

1. When a seed is buried in warm, moist soil, it...

2. Each little seed contains all the information...

3. The seed must shrivel up and die...

4. Germination means that...

5. The Bible describes...

6. The facts of science...

...will soon germinate.

...this process accurately.

...needed to form a new plant.

...always agree with God's Word.

...the seed produces a root and a shoot.

...as its inner cells are used to support new life!

In **John 12:24** Jesus said ....
....
....
....

Life from Life

The Bible teaches (Genesis 1) that the first animals to live on the earth were created by God. God made many different types of animals, which would look, sound and behave in wonderfully different ways! Zoologists are still making exciting new discoveries about some animal habits.

Bones, muscles, skin and blood vessels cannot become a living creature all by themselves...so the *living* God gave life to the first animals. When an animal gives birth, life is then passed from one living body to the next. Scientists today are agreed that life can only come from existing life* . . . which is just what the Bible describes.

Can you match each adult bird or animal to its baby?

dog
swan
bear
deer
goose
frog
hare
goat
elephant
puppy
gosling
cub
fawn
kid
tadpole
calf
leveret
cygnet

*see page 32

Different Kinds

Within every species of animal there is amazing variety. Mice, for example, can be found in many different colours, shapes and sizes.

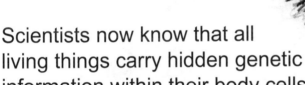

But everyone knows that a mouse will only give birth to a baby mouse! A cat can never have a puppy, and a hippo will never produce a lion-cub!

Scientists now know that all living things carry hidden genetic information within their body cells. This information determines what they look like but also makes it impossible for them to breed with an animal which has a different genetic make-up. So mice can only be the parents of more mice! The Bible says God planned this from the beginning!

Genesis 1:24 says...

....

....

Can you rearrange these words to make true statements?

Mice be in shapes and colours many and found can sizes

....

A never cat can a birth puppy to give

....

God that said creature every produce after would own his kind

....

Dinosaurs

The **first** chapter of the Bible teaches that God created the land **animals** on the **same** day as he made the first man. So that includes **dinosaurs**!

Many fossilized **skeletons** have been found, proving that these amazing creatures **did** exist, but they didn't roam the earth millions of years ago. The Bible describes an earth which is only **thousands**, not millions, of years old (eg. consider Genesis 5).

So why don't we find the word 'dinosaur' in the Bible? The reason is that it's really quite a **new** word. It was invented in 1842 by a scientist called Sir Richard Owen, when he unearthed some fossilized bones belonging to **huge** reptiles. 'Dinosaur' simply means 'terrible lizard'.

The Bible was translated into English in the 1600s, and often uses the word '**dragon**' to describe this type of creature. Many people believe that the majestic beast described in Job 40:15-24 could well have been a large sauropod.

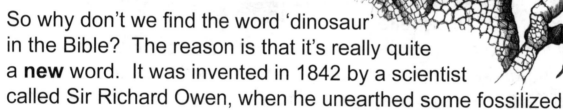

Can you fit the words in bold letters into the grid?

Fossils Everywhere!

Have you ever been digging in the .... or near the beach and found a fossil? It looks just like a twig, or a shell, or maybe the bone of an animal, but it is made of ....

If an animal dies in the usual way the body smells terrible as it .... and decomposes (rots away). Fresh air is needed for the rotting to take place quickly. But if an animal is buried in wet bogland this rotting may .... happen at all. Amazing things have been found in boglands, in almost perfect condition, centuries .... they were first buried!

Fossils are formed when animals or .... are buried quickly, and deeply, in wet conditions, without oxygen, before they had enough time to decay or decompose. We find them all over the world, and sometimes we even find fossils of creatures which are no .... living on the earth and are now extinct, eg. dinosaurs.

We shouldn't be at all

....

to find lots of fossils in so many places because God's Word describes a terrible world-wide event which caused the sudden burial of millions of animal bodies in very wet conditions!

It was known as The Flood and it happened in the days of Noah. You can read about it in **Genesis chapters 6 and 7.**

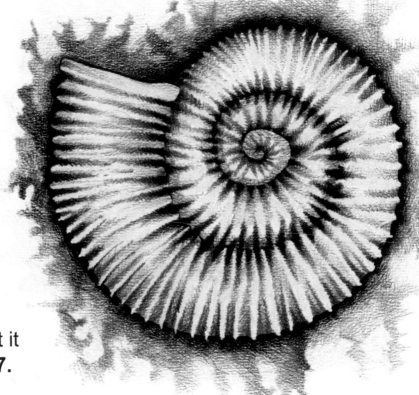

The Best Design

No-one really knows what the **ark**, built by **Noah** and his sons, actually looked like. But we do know that it was 300 cubits long (a cubit is about 18 inches or 46 centimetres), 50 cubits wide and 30 cubits deep.

Scientists have carried out some experiments, to find out what shape of boat **floats** best. When models of twelve other ships, with different dimensions but similar

S	O	N	G	I	S	E	D	U	K
E	C	G	O	W	F	N	O	T	R
V	T	I	B	U	S	B	I	M	A
U	S	T	E	D	A	I	Y	D	E
S	E	R	H	N	U	B	A	E	R
T	B	S	O	L	T	L	G	T	E
A	E	A	C	E	S	I	A	S	N
O	H	F	R	A	U	C	S	E	O
L	A	E	T	I	R	A	I	T	P
F	W	S	K	O	T	L	U	W	S

volumes to the ark, were **tested**, none was found to be quite so **safe** as the **design** God first gave to Noah. In conditions of severe storm the boat with the **best** combination of comfort, stability and strength was the **biblical** ark.* We can always **trust** God's Word absolutely!

The words written in bold letters are hidden in the wordsearch. Can you find them?

see page 32

Just as God Said!

We've had the complete Bible for about 1900 years. It was authored by God the Creator and is an utterly reliable book. The more we discover about 'earthly things' the more we find them to be 'just as God said'.

God has said some other very important things too. In the Bible he has told us that all the people on earth are sinful compared to his holiness.

In **Romans 3:23** we read ....
....

God is also just, so he must punish all sin. But he didn't leave us without a way of escape. Out of his great love for mankind he sent his only Son, Jesus Christ, into the world, to take the punishment for our sin.

In **John 3:16** we read ....
....
....

God has promised that if we turn from our sins, and receive and rest upon the Lord Jesus Christ, we will be forgiven. The Bible teaches that God gives eternal life to all who believe on the name of his Son.

1 John 5:11-12 says.....
....
....
....
....
....
....
....
....
....

Notes for adults . . .

page 3
Stark, R., *For the Glory of God: How Monotheism Led to Reformations, Science, Witch-hunts, and the End of Slavery* (Princeton University Press, 2003), p. 165.

page 26
The Law of Biogenesis states that life can only come from life.

page 30
www.worldwideflood.com/ark/hull_form/hull_optimization.htm

Acknowledgements
I am indebted to both Answers in Genesis and Creation Ministries International for the helpful resources they continue to produce, which have, over the years, encouraged in our children a steady confidence in the Word of God.